THE ZIONESS' DEN

FRUIT OF THE SPIRIT EDITION

AN ADVANCED *MY TIME WITH THE MOST HIGH* WORKBOOK

PART TWO

BY

TARA LA SEAN

The Lord's Prayer

Our Father (Ahayah) which art in Heaven, Hallowed be thy name. Thy kingdom come, Thy will be done in earth, as it is in Heaven. Give us this day our daily bread. And forgive us our debts as we forgive our debtors. And lead us not into temptation, but deliver us from evil: For thine is the kingdom, and the power, and the glory, forever.

Ahayah Bahasham Yashaya Wa Rawach

(In the name of the Father, the Son and the Holy Spirit)

Amen

Shalom Brothers and Sisters!

It gives me great pleasure to present this latest segment of the *My Time With The Most High* workbook series! Much like the other books in this series, The Zioness' Den: Fruit of the Spirit Edition features a variety of puzzles, writing prompts and other activities designed to help learners identify those attributes of the Holy Spirit we should all strive for. While the lessons are focused on how girls and women of our generation should apply the understanding of the Fruit into our lives by using the stellar women of the Bible as examples, I encourage our Ahchyam (brothers) to also work through the lessons, as they can learn much as well.

Although this series features many of same types of activities as the original and can be used by learners of all ages, *The Zioness' Den* is geared toward more advanced students. To complete the activities in this section you will need the KJV Bible, The Apocrypha and the Book of Jasher (as translated by R.H. Charles).* This section assumes that you have read these records and are at least familiar with the content.

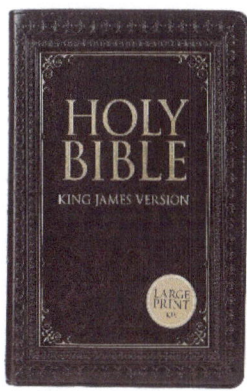

I hope you will continue to study the Word and learn more about our Magnificent Power, Ahayah, as well as the Rawach Qadash as presented in the Fruit of the Spirit!

Barak Atha!

Sis Tara~

*If you do not have these records by R.H. Charles, you can download them for free as a PDF to your personal device. http://www.parsontom.com/books/Book%20of%20Jasher.pdf

** The Apocrypha can also be found in the 1611 KJV Bible

THE PERFECT PORTRAIT OF GOODNESS

LEAH THE LOVING

SUSANNA THE STALWART

REBEKKA THE RIGHTEOUS

Its Good to be GOOD!

Complete the crossword puzzle below using the KJV to solve the clues.

Across
3. TMH can make all grace abound toward you and all _____ in all things.
4. Instead of placing a candle under a bushel, we place it on this to give light to the whole room.
5. What does evil communications do to good manners?
7. 1 Pet. 3 teaches that if we follow good, none can do this ___ to us.
8. TMH is this ___ in the day of trouble and He knows them that trust Him. (2 words)

Down
1. Let love be without this ____.
2. Ps. 34 says we should seek and pursue this ___ as we turn from evil and do good.
6. Ahayah is ____ in all His ways and holy in all His works.

But Do I L👁️👁️K Good, though?

In today's world there is much emphasis on how a woman looks. Sisters spend a fortune on their hair, nails, clothes and shoes and will often forego investing in their education, business opportunities or even paying bills to have the latest celeb-endorsed "look." Let's read 1 Tim. 2:9-10 carefully. What does this passage say about how a woman should present herself? Also explain how this scripture relates to the fruit Goodness. Be sure to include at least two precepts to support your answer.

Finding the Good in All Things

From the very beginning the Alahayam has shown goodness in every way imaginable. Unfortunately, in today's world we sometimes lose sight of all the splendor and beauty around us. Let's take a look at a just a few categories in which The Most High has shown us His Goodness. In each of the categories below, find at least three scriptures (in different areas of the Word) to remind us of that goodness.

The Goodness of Creation

The Goodness of Salvation

The Goodness of Ahayah

The Goodness of Family

Sisters in the Background

Complete the crossword puzzle below. Use the KJV Bible to answer the clues!

Created using the Crossword Maker on TheTeachersCorner.n

Across

1. Devoted, hardworking, trustworthy woman of the early Church in Cenchrea who delivered Paul's letter to the Romans.

4. New testament wife who worked with her husband and the Apostle to the Gentles in both the ministry and in business.

7. Hardworking sibling of Mary and Lazarus in the New Testament-

8. New Testament woman known for doing good and helping the poor

9. Second daughter of Job who inherited from her father, a practice that was still uncommon at during that era.

Down

2. Two faith women who were part of the early Church and mother and grandmother to the Apostle Timothy (3 words).

3. Written of in the book of Mark, this third "Mary" was a disciple of Yashaya who followed him to his crucifixion and one of the women who found the tomb empty.

5. This New Testament servant girl was so overjoyed at the return of Peter from prison, that in her haste to tell the others she didn't open the gate.

6. Old testament woman whose faith inspired her son's young widow to choose the God of Israel and follow her to her homeland.

8

REAL SISTERS; REAL FAITH

"And fear not them which kill the body, but are not able to kill the soul: but rather fear him which is able to destroy both soul and body in hell." Matt. 10:28

Shiphrah & Puah delivering Jochabed

Defining Faith

Hebrews Chapter 11 is known as the "faith chapter." In it, we can see many examples of faith at work and get a strong understanding of this important word. Starting with the Hebrew word for faith, write out the definition given by Strong's. Give five scriptural examples of faith from this chapter and how it can be used and exercised in our walk with Ahayah.

Example 1:
_____
_____
_____
_____
_____

Example 2:
_____
_____
_____
_____
_____

Example 3:
_____
_____
_____
_____
_____

Example 4:
_____
_____
_____
_____
_____

Example 5:
_____
_____
_____
_____

Women operating in Faith

Throughout scripture there are accounts of men and women who were very strong in the Faith and exhibited it in many ways. Today, we will focus of five such sisters who kept their hearts focused on Ahayah and did wonderful things to help their families and all of Israel. Read the following stories and explain what they did and why it is an example of faith. Be sure to include at least one precept to support your answer.

Jochebed Ex. 2:

_____
_____
_____
_____
_____
_____

Huldah 2 Kings 22:

_____
_____
_____
_____
_____
_____

Hannah 1 Sam. 1:

_____
_____
_____
_____
_____
_____

Puah and Shiphrah Ex. 1:

_____
_____
_____
_____

It's All About Faith!

Complete the crossword puzzle below using clues from passages in the KJV Bible.

Across
3. What did Mother Sara receive by faith to conceive in the book of Hebrews?
5. Whatsoever is born of Ahayah _____ the world by faith. 1 John
6. In faith, what type of fight should we have according to 1 Tim.? (2 words)
8. Word in Heb. 11 that gives us the 'proof' of our faith.
9. He who does this '_____' is like a wave of the sea driven with the wind...
10. What does faith replace in our walk according to 2 Cor. 5?

Down
1. By faith, this happened to Enoch so the he did not see death.
2. Ephesians teaches that by _____ we are saved through faith.
4. According to the Apostle Mark, what is the key to receiving what you pray for?
7. Which of the senses does faith come by?

Would You Believe?

All through the Bible we find several scriptures linking faith to belief. By now I'm sure we can all agree that a large part of *faith* is to *believe*. Go through both the Old and New Testaments and find scriptures about faith/belief. Write down the verse and explain what it means. Advanced students should be able to link the verse to at least one other precept!

Verse 1: Example

Ps. 20:7 "Some trust in chariots, and some in horses: but we will remember the name of the LORD our God." Explained: Some people have faith (trust) in weapons and material things for protection, but I place my trust in the name of Yashaya. Precept: Luke 10:17 Even the devils are subject to the power that is his name.

Verse 2:

_____
_____
_____

Verse 3:

_____
_____
_____

Verse 4:

_____
_____
_____

Verse 5:

_____
_____
_____

Verse 6:

_____
_____
_____

Ruth; The Meek

"Blessed are the meek: for they shall inherit the earth." Matt. 5:5

Meekness: A Key to Feminine Perfection

When you hear the word "meek," what type of person comes to mind? Until I began studying the Word I thought being meek meant to be wimpy and a push-over; someone who lacked a back-bone or the ability to stand up for themselves. In short; a person who is easily taken advantage of. But let's examine how Ahayah defines being meek and why we should aspire to be this way. Let's begin with a definition study in order to fully understand what it means to be "meek." Look up the words and definitions for the following Strong's Hebrew and Greek numbers and write the word and definition. Next, we'll review the story of our sister Ruth and discuss how she exhibited this fruit in various situations.

Part I

1. H6035

   _____
   _____

2. G5012

   _____
   _____

3. G4239

   _____
   _____

4. H3665

   _____
   _____

5. G5218

   _____
   _____

6. H3349

   _____
   _____

Part II

1. **How did Ruth show meekness in the fields of Boaz?**

   _____

   _____

   _____

2. **How did she exemplify meekness on the threshing floor?**

   _____

   _____

   _____

3. **How did her relationship with Naomi show her meekness?**

   _____

   _____

   _____

4. **Explain how obedience and humility relates to being meek:**

   _____

   _____

   _____

Meek is Chic!

Throughout these lessons we have discussed how the world teaches women that being meek and humble is to be weak and that we should be brazen, loud and full of vanity. Let's read the following passages and discuss what each one says about being meek and why being righteous and meek is always "en vogue"!

1. **Col. 3:12**

2. **James 4:6**

3. **Ps. 149:4**

4. **Eph. 4:2**

5. **Luke 14:11**

6. **Prov. 18:12**

7. **Ps. 25:9**

8. **Rom. 12:16**

LOW, MEEK AND HUMBLE IS THE WAY!

As Daughters of Zion, we have learned the importance of being meek and humble. However, we may still struggle to exhibit these characteristics in various areas of our lives. Review the following scriptures and determine which of the following relationship categories we can apply the passage to.

Towards Ahayah ~ Towards Parents ~ Toward Husbands ~ Towards Others

1. Rom. 12:16
   _____

2. 1 Pet. 5:6
   _____

3. 1 Pet. 3:8
   _____

4. Phil. 2:3
   _____

5. Matt. 6:2
   _____

6. Col. 3:18-19
   _____

7. Gal. 5:13
   _____

8. Jam. 4:10
   _____

9. Prov. 22:4
   _____

10. 2 Chron. 7:14
    _____

Temperance

Manoah's Wife: A True Example of Gentle Temperance

Manoah's Wife: When Gentleness and Temperance Met

Though she is unnamed in the scriptures, this woman left a beautiful example of how a wife should be both gentle and temperate. Read Judges 13 and pay close attention to verse 23. Discuss how she was an example of gentleness and temperance. Also discuss how, if this had been a modern situation, the "world" would have influenced her to react to her husband differently. Finally, search out 3-5 precepts on how a wife should be towards her husband and how Manoah's wife fit the passage.

 Bee Creative

Although temperance is one of the Fruit of the Spirit, it seems to be one of the least-studied attributes of the Spirit. However, understanding this trait and how to apply it to our lives is vastly important. Let's begin by looking up both the Strong's Hebrew and Greek words for temperance along with the definition. In many ways, the world teaches girls/ women that being temperate is undesirable and we should behave in opposition of this Fruit. In the space below, draw a picture, write a poem or make up a story highlighting the behaviors the world encourages women to practice.

The Sheer Beauty of Self-Restraint

As Daughters of Zion we sometimes overlook the importance of being temperate in all aspects of our lives. Let's spend a few minutes reading the following scriptures and matching them to the area of our lives the passages are referring to from the list. Then, describe how *you* either exemplify temperance in this area or how you *should* incorporate this principle in your daily life. Add at least *one* precept to each answer.

Matthew 18:15   Ecclesiasticus 2:4   Prov. 25:16   Heb. 13:17   Col. 3:23   Prov. 4:23

Temperance in our *Bodies*:
___
___
___

Temperance in our *Minds*:
___
___
___

Temperance in our *Relationships*:
___
___
___

Temperance on our *Jobs/ School*:
___
___
___

Temperance in the *Church*:
___
___
___

Temperance in our *Attitudes*:
___
___
___

Gossip Girls...

At the beginning of this section on temperance I challenged you all to **Bee Creative** and discuss what behaviors are encouraged by the world that goes against the Spirit of Ahayah. While there are several out there, the act of gossiping is definitely one of the most destructive. When we are not being temperate in what we say or in what we listen to, we are inviting trouble into our lives. Read the following passages carefully and explain how it relates to temperance. Then give an example of a possible consequence for not heeding the scripture.

Prov. 18:21
_____
_____

Eph. 4:29
_____
_____

Prov. 18:8
_____
_____

James 1:26
_____
_____

Prov. 10:19
_____
_____

Prov. 16:28
_____
_____

1 Timothy 5:13-14
_____
_____

Oh, to be temperate like her...

Below you will find a group of three women in each section. Choose the **one** sister from **each** section who you think was the best example of temperance. Be sure to give at least two examples of how they exuded this fruit and at least two scriptures to support your answer.

Sara, Leah, Rebekah

_____
_____
_____
_____
_____
_____
_____
_____
_____
_____

Susanna, Judith, Mama Macabee

_____
_____
_____
_____
_____
_____
_____
_____
_____
_____

Phoebe, Mary of Bethany, Priscilla

_____
_____
_____
_____
_____
_____
_____
_____
_____
_____

Now let's add a little Patience…

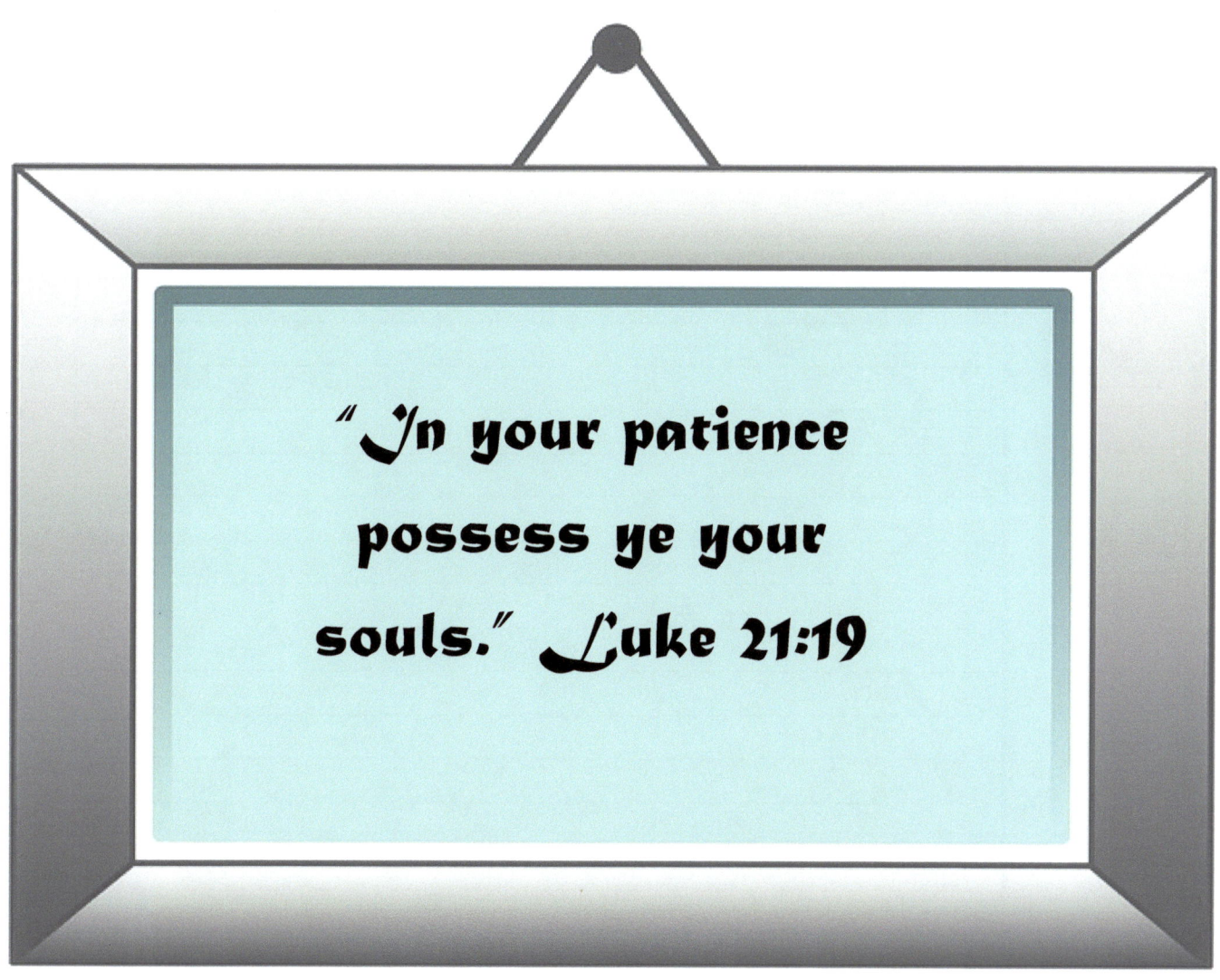

"In your patience possess ye your souls." Luke 21:19

Patience and Faith; A Double Fruit Delight!

Romans 8:25 gives us a glimpse into the relationship between faith and patience. "But if we hope for that we see not, then do we with patience wait for it." Examine what this passage says about this relationship and explain how these two "fruits" work together. Make sure you include at least three other precepts in your answer.

PATIENCE IS A VIRTUE...

All of our lives we've heard the expression "patience is a virtue." But have you ever sat down and really examined what patience is or what it really means? Let's begin by looking up the Strong's Hebrew and Greek words for patience and compare how the two are used in the Old and New Testaments. Review the precepts below and explain how the word being used in the passage relates to patience.

1. Strong's Hebrew word and definition:

2. Strong's Greek word and definition:

3. Rom. 5:3

4. Prov. 14:29

5. Gal. 6:9

6. Ex. 14:14

7. 2 Pet. 3:9

8. Luke 8:15

9. 2 Cor. 1:6

10. Prov. 16:32

12 Words of Patience
Find the words in the puzzle below.

FORBEARANCE
PERTINACITY
ENDURANCE
CALMNESS

TOLERANCE
CONSIDERATION
UNDERSTANDING
DILIGENCE

SERENITY
RESTRAINT
TRANQUILITY
RESOLUTE

And At the Heart of the Fruit is...

After studying the nine fruit of the spirit, chose which one you think is at the center of them all. Write that fruit in the heart below and show how it connects to the other eight fruit. Be sure to include at least one precept in your answer and give an example of how your chosen fruit supports the next fruit. Ex.: If faith is at the heart how does it connect to peace, joy, love, etc.

Shalom Family,

I pray that you all have enjoyed the second half of the ***Zioness' Den: Fruit of the Spirit Edition.*** It is always a blessing to share the lessons I am learning with my family! I must confess, I really felt the studies on Longsuffering and Temperance and will undoubtedly dig deeper into these two fruit.

As I have said in previous books, my purpose is not to actually "teach" the Bible, but to offer a guide for self-study. It is my sincere prayer that all our young people (in age and spirit) will develop a love and passion for spending time with the Father through reading the Word, prayer and reflection/ meditation. As this is not an actual textbook, there is no formal grading rubric and with the exception of the puzzles, there are no right or wrong answers. Having said that, the writing assignments can be done verbally or used to spark discussion among a class or family unit. Unlike the ***My Time With The Most High*** series, target grade levels for this series is eighth grade and up as this is a more advanced series. However, the writing assignments can be expanded for older students and shortened for the younger ones. Feel free to manipulate the prompts and activities to suit your needs. The main point is to get into the Word daily!

I must make a note about how the materials were put together. Both the photographers and models are part of my church family and have agreed to help in this endeavor by portraying these incredible women (thawadah ladies and the Audio/ Visual Ministry!). Also, many of the puzzles were generated through TheTeachersCorner.net. but the content is from the Holy Bible; KJV. With that said, I hope you have enjoyed the activities!

Barak Athan,

Sis. Tara

Answers

Its Good to be GOOD!

Complete the crossword puzzle below using the KJV to solve the clues.

Across

3. TMH can make all grace abound toward you and all _____ in all things. (**sufficiency**)
4. Instead of placing a candle under a bushel, we place it on this to give light to the whole room. (**candlestick**)
5. What does evil communications do to good manners? (**corrupt**)
7. 1 Pet. 3 teaches that if we follow good, none can do this ___ to us. (**harm**)
8. TMH is this ___ in the day of trouble and He knows them that trust Him. (2 words) (**strong hold**)

Down

1. Let love be without this ____. (**dissimulation**)
2. Ps. 34 says we should seek and pursue this ___ as we turn from evil and do good. (**peace**)
6. Ahayah is ____ in all His ways and holy in all His works. (**righteous**)

Sisters in the Background

Complete the crossword puzzle below. Use the KJV Bible to answer the clues!

Across
1. Devoted, hardworking, trustworthy woman of the early Church in Cenchrea who delivered Paul's letter to the Romans. (**phoebe**)
4. New testament wife who worked with her husband and the Apostle to the Gentiles in both the ministry and in business. (**priscilla**)
7. Hardworking sibling of Mary and Lazarus in the New Testament- (**martha**)
8. New Testament woman known for going good and helping the poor (**tabitha**)
9. Second daughter of Job who inherited from her father, a practice that was still uncommon at during that era. (**keziah**)

Down
2. Two faith women who were part of the early Church and mother and grandmother to the Apostle Timothy (3 words). (**eunice and lois**)
3. Written of in the book of Mark, this third "Mary" was a disciple of Yashaya who followed him to his crucifixion and one of th (**salome**)
5. This New Testament servant girl was so overjoyed at the return of the Apostle Peter from prison, that in her haste to tell th (**rhoda**)
6. Old testament woman whose faith inspired her son's young widow to choose the God of Israel and follow her to her homeland. (**naomi**)

Created using the Crossword Maker on TheTeachersCorner.net

It's All About Faith!
Complete the crossword puzzle below using clues from passages in the KJV Bible.

Across

3. What did Mother Sara receive by faith to conceive in the book of Hebrews? (**strength**)
5. Whatsoever is born of Ahayah _____ the world by faith. 1 John (**overcometh**)
6. In faith, what type of fight should we have according to 1 Tim.? (2 words) (**good fight**)
8. Word in Heb. 11 that gives us the 'proof' of our faith. (**evidence**)
9. He who does this '_____' is like a wave of the sea driven with the wind... (**wavers**)
10. What does faith replace in our walk according to 2 Cor. 5? (**sight**)

Down

1. By faith, this happened to Enoch so the he did not see death. (**translated**)
2. Ephesians teaches that by _____ we are saved through faith. (**grace**)
4. According to the Apostle Mark, what is the key to receiving what you pray for? (**believing**)
7. Which of the senses does faith come by? (**hearing**)

12 Words of Patience
Find the words in the puzzle below.

```
C V K V T D P E W Z V Y V S U K N N O G
A E N D U R A N C E T L N Q M S R E K F
L Z E Q R O V T P I N I X Q R X I G I G
M Q U C G V P L L E F Q L R Y N X C U E
N X F Y N T K I M Y R E Z L Z C B P R C
E O S S I A U L Q F C T W G E F Q N J N
S C I Z D Q R M O G A P I I R G E W Y R
S C C T N Y Z A P Q W J F N M D U C W L
W U F A A I U U E I K T E W A E B T X V
W M R L T R W A I B R S I K O C Y C I A
W T X I S W E D Q J R L D C J N I C W Y
A R K B R F A D U L P O J X K E F T V W
L E V H E Q J H I U S D F Q C G K B Y U
V S O D D W N Z N S L E D C A I S S W U
E T K Q N U E H K C N K R V A L A J H S
E R K E U B P V L D U O J E E I P L J T
K A X T O L E R A N C E C V N D U A W D
S I W W W M D R Q Z N H D D Z I X M A W
J N F X P S Q L E T U L O S E R T B V Y
U T E P I M S S L Y R R X R U D R Y X S
```

FORBEARANCE	TOLERANCE	SERENITY
PERTINACITY	CONSIDERATION	RESTRAINT
ENDURANCE	UNDERSTANDING	TRANQUILITY
CALMNESS	DILIGENCE	RESOLUTE

www.ingramcontent.com/pod-product-compliance
Lightning Source LLC
Chambersburg PA
CBHW042029150426
43198CB00003B/104